A SECOND

GW01459827

A Second Life

WILLIAM SCAMMELL

HARRY CHAMBERS/PETERLOO POETS

First published in 1982
by Harry Chambers/Peterloo Poets
Treovis Farm Cottage, Upton Cross, Liskeard, Cornwall PL14 5BQ

ISBN 0 905291 38 7

Printed in Great Britain by
Latimer Trend & Company Ltd, Plymouth

ACKNOWLEDGEMENTS are due to the editors of *Bananas, Critical Quarterly, The Honest Ulsterman, The Listener, London Magazine, PEN Broadsheet, Poetry Review* and *Times Literary Supplement,* in whose pages some of these poems first appeared.

'Monday, Monday', 'The Road' and 'Upstairs' were broadcast on *Poetry Now* (BBC Radio 3).

'A Day in the Country' first appeared, in a slightly different form, in *New Poetry 6* (Arts Council/PEN), edited by Ted Hughes.

The sequence *Time Past* was first published in a limited edition by Treovis Press (1982).

Harry Chambers/Peterloo Poets receives financial assistance from The Arts Council of Great Britain.

Contents

Monday, Monday

The auctioneer's a diva. From his shed
Hi pinny ped! Hi pinny ped!

floats out in aria. One cow do blink,
the packed-in squares of Herdwicks pool their stink

while capped and gaitered shepherds, taking in
exotic species such as me, drink gin

and bitter in the all-day-open pubs
deploring this year's weather and the barmaid's bubs.

Three hefty ladies in the bakers' chat
of death, disaster, Mrs Newbold's hat

and Tessa's canny wedding. Over in ANTIQUES
Miss Cooper dusts the Romneys, shoos her pekes

from off the Persians, glances up to see
the High Street ticking and a ghostly eye

in POET'S CORNER, where old dummies leer
across the decades in their classic gear.

The bank is humming. Sealed off behind glass
the clerks munch paper, and the Big Moustache

sits down to business. Where there's muck there too's
the pinstripe and the polished shoes,

the furrowed brows of farmers, who will keep
and pasture prejudice, as they do sheep.

I'm just an idler; he's a narrow brute
whose mind is laced up in his boot . . .

But on the bridge, where placid Derwent slows
the racy stride of Cocker, we touch nose

at one another as we pass, sniff hard
respectively, the blank sheet and the knackers yard.

The Road

The road runs straight, like Hadrian's Wall
nearby. Out in the wind, between coast
and coast, a half-used land, spectacular
wide-lidded skies, the sun's eye
balancing on cars. What blows through
is placelessness, the mother-stuff
you couldn't live with. Immanence
is all to do again, whether the heel-stamp
of a Roman god, or mocking waves
from jiggly severed hands in lorry cabs.

The Vet

'You know I'm not going out again'
shaking me fiercely with his eye. I knew
and watched him grappling. When his sleeves rode up
he twitched them down again, hands huge
against a workman's wasted arms.
His face was like a hunter's, crowded
with one sharp thought. Dull bottles
glittered round. 'If I was a dog
I'd have myself put down.' Once more
the stare, which travelled further than the joke.
We talked of night-time: not
to open one last scrip of days. Sometimes
he watched the jingles on TV: the eyelids
tissued down . . . Time funnelled to his eyes
and froze there, jointed like tossed hair
the camera frames and slows. He practised
being dead; the eyes would grip and grip.

Snow at the funeral: snow and wind,
a tiny coffin. All his life was light.

Moving

We shift about like gypsies: ten
or twelve addresses in a dozen years.

Pictures lord it over plain white walls
bringing the outside inside, reminding
the present of its ancestry. Chairs, tables,
beds resume old servitudes, shabby—
comfy as house-serfs in *War and Peace*.

Listening to the growl of cars,
the soft tick of my watch.

Love is away up the road
a glissando of cc's.

How to Derive an Ought from an Is

For my retiring skeleton
has several wishes; one of them
is grisly, but the other three
pad up and down my vertebrae

like creamy long pacific waves
that in their sedentary stride
have burnished islands, fed each coast
with captain, playboy, poet, priest.

Hostages

The boys are playing snooker on the small
table that greens half their room. Paddington,
Tarzan, Charlie's Angels, Liverpool
('Champions of Europe'), the Bionic Man,

phantoms off the deck of the *Ark Royal*,
British birds, freshwater fish, and dinosaurs
inhabit the bedroom walls in archaeological
layers stretching back to Eden, when pure

and tasteful colours lullabyed bright eyes
and love was all in all. But now the mind
grows fat on novelty, riots in surprise
as on the cassette tape the Beatles climb

to uproar and nirvana. 'Give me one
good reason why I should go to bed!' I spring
amongst the colours of revolt, waving a gun
at chaos. Civilisation's setting in.

A Day In The Country

The tide of green laps to the window-box:
Miss Smith is delivered of a tawny rose,

West London shot to pieces by a plant.
O that scrumptious English landscape where

the books are cooked, tradition gorging
at each eye. Released, the psyche runs

to minty clouds and drystone walls, a mild and bitter
in those dolls-house pubs old soldiers bull

and buckle on them like Achilles' shield.
Rooks, high in their asylum, fling out

clouds of swear-words, settling anathemas
on each nest; gargoyles swallow at old

ticklish jokes; weathercocks heel on gold.
Good breeding worms its taproot

where the riddle diced and shook down
darkness to a nursery quilt.

Praetorian nettles fan out round each farm;
someone's grafting rainbows, deep-thighed

where the levels brim.

Bliss

I

Let's go to bed—we've drunk enough
to rinse the alphabet of love;
and see if our two bodies can
construe the oldest lexicon.
You're fat and forty, I'm as thin
as charity on Monday morning.
No no, that's hyperbolic: you're
just nicely ample and mature,
aesthetically wired, your nerves
a bright baroque of solid curves.
Those black silk pants, voluminous,
Betjemanic-numinous
you carelessly fling to the ground
articulate a holy sound.
The mind grows rich: this union
will put me up with Solomon
and Joseph Smith, while Rochester
grows greener in his sepulchre.
In you all women meet, and I
am happy to burn out and die
in one impossible embrace
of all the runners in the race.
Thus I fatten up my pain
and lead it to the block again
and you, in taking me to bed,
are dieting the maidenhead
of your immortal soul, which feeds
on pure imaginary deeds.
The sheets impart a deathly chill,
salting our raw wounds; yet still
we'll kick into the solid dark
that ticks against the window, mark
the distance in a first slow kiss,
swallow down our proper bliss,
talk or smoke, curl up, two hooks
disposed in quiet questionmarks.

II

A party. Cheap wine, lots of beer,
loud music, baked potatoes. Clear
distractions in each swivelled head
to sort the living from the dead.
This one was folksy—ethnic types
in waistcoats, baggy trousers, pipes,
large girls in dingy brown, adrift
on cider, bonhomie and thrift.
Then steals in one from Amsterdam
like Ariel to a rugger scrum,
slender as a choirboy, trussed
in tight jeans, skinny sweater, bust
just marginally present as
a smutch of incense at high mass.
O gamine, 1920s fine,
my flapper girl, my androgyne!
If Greeks aspired to this, to speak
of nature's best, then I'm a Greek.
Such narrow polished shoulders, arms
like tulip stems, a waist whose charms
flash out between the plimsoll line
of calculated denim, fine
ribbed sweater dyed the shade of blood,
and hips like Bambi's. O what would
I give to metamorphose you
in words as literally true
as your pale face which, tilting, smiles
into my eyes for miles and miles
unlocking all the grisly chains
devised for hope by my small brains!
Come then; that tragic smile will be
our mute and golden sesame:
in bed we'll nibble, minnow-like,
at tongue and teeth, the very type
and soul of perfect lovers who
ascend the food-chain as they chew.

Solemn, slender, graceful, poised
in anguish like an insect, joy's
what grips your water-boatman limbs
and rides the turbulence within.
My God, your gift was guilt; here is
the acme of antithesis,
ripe knowledge at the shallow core
of my Shakespearian boy-girl whore
whose ragged fringe conceals such eyes
as turn the locks in paradise.

—Amen. There's coffee down below.
And look, the dawn is dark with snow.

Polyhaemia

Bald, stinking, wrinkled—mark the Queen
her breast deep-frozen in brocade.
Blood lechers still in every vein
commanding coxcombs ply their trade.

Straddling the seas in courtly love
her ports and inlets mapped for use
Britannia summons favours of
her favourites, for self-abuse.

I too stood next her once. She wore
a throb of musk on hectic skin
and waved her maids out at the door
and eyed me with her famishing.

Crazed with power, she simpers by
among her sworded gallants, hums
a snatch of my old lyric cry
stirring her fleet of gorgeous bums.

Time Past

I. THE KITCHEN

Engines! where the florid copper boiled up, shook
a scalding finger at the least mistake,

my Mother a mad tympanist, alert-
ly thundering the *Götterdämmerung* of dirt.

Hair-triggered, rancid, black, the frying pan
gunned sausages, exploding kidneys like a bomb;

and Father stropped his cut-throat; and the roast
saw Sunday to its knees, as well as Christ.

Cursing, Dad roughed out soles with knife and rasp,
hammering sole to upper on the last

and Ma wrought celtic crosses, bleeding hearts,
illuminating moon-faced apple tarts.

(My treat was raw sweet rags of dough, chewed small,
or sealing the pungent hide with hot heel-ball.)

Some sort of steam was always flowering there
if only shouts and curses. 'I don't care!'

was answered by 'I do!' and all the rage
of finer feelings under family siege

till want of space, attention, money, beer,
condensed to a humped back, or slamming door.

The kettle sang a mantra on its fire;
three Buddhist teapots nodded out the hour.

2. LIVING ROOM

Dad humped it in and moored it by the fire;
steam shot off tilting buckets like a funeral pyre.

Stripped nude and skinny, stepping into air:
bath night, with Palm Court angels on the Home,

Mum's towel going at an oedipal four-four.
You peeled your bottom off the tin

like an elastoplast, then stuck your
sizzling curls out at the fire's high din

and boiled them dry, while devil gymnasts
fizzed along the fender's liquid brass.

Exploring, once I trekked to our front room
and squandered all our sharing, flung

the capital of space away to sit
in adamantine cold and get things right.

3. THE SHED

Large spiders, arcane reading to be had
and pondered in the outside bucket lav.

Damp brick ate up the whitewash; lintels sagged,
gnawed slowly down to ash. Old Raleighs wagged

shin-raking pedals at a junk of coal;
black webs and rags of webbing swagged each wall.

Coal, wood, bike-oil, sacks, spongy papers, shit,
soft dizzy spores of dark: you throned in it.

4. UPSTAIRS

I tried my Mother's bracelets on at ten
and gashed my lips a Clara Bow vermilion.

Matchless, the naked act of one's own face
regressing in the curtains of the glass.

Could seeing be observed, might I distil
a face beneath my faces, touch the will

crouched deep inside the petals of the flesh,
light clinging to the pearl strand at my breast?

As I leant to the mirror, eye to eye,
the room closed up behind, stared back at me

with tall shut polished cupboards, nameless clouds
of fallen dust and perfumes, patterned shrouds.

Oak drawers, deep as secrets, slid out wide;
silk foamed up on my wrists. The widening tide

of quiet drove me from the strip of red
and ruined carpet, that high double bed.

5. MANDRAKE

Plantaganet and peasant, on the job
six nights a week, my Father ruled the workmen's club

where twelve-pint-men grew weighty at the bar
and billiard balls rolled peacably to war.

He'd married it, my Mother said. 'That man
'ud be as happy with a frying pan!'

She took in Irish lodgers, slaved and queued,
half in love with epic rectitude;

paid all the bills, complained, perfected looks
more dense than lovers' vows in library books.

The card-school pondered, two by two; 'young Janes'
(Ma's withering label) tilted babychams

and little fingers, gathering muscle for
the leap from maidenhood to bottom drawer.

My choices still have genders: cosy-sad
back home with Mum, or packing straight to hell with Dad.

6. EACH TO EACH

My first bookcase was tacked up on the wall
beside my bed. All my decline and fall

from that ferocious nest of amity
was signalled in the Penguin *Odyssey*

and other classics lovingly aligned
by height, shape, colour, author; and I signed

my name in each to make it clear
that culture was for keeps. This solemn year

the room was all my own.—So was my head.
I served it on a platter to the dead.

The Duel

Millions of tons of light
crouches on snow.
The horses snort like engines.

Comme il faut
in a January field
bathed and perfumed as for a ball
or an affair, two stand
watching. Natalya

most beautiful and stupid
is at home
wearing her crystal shoulders
down to breakfast;
while honour, armed and booted,
waits to stain the ground
with motive.

Pushkin's down; the other
turns to go.
'Wait!'
D'Anthès stands, folding
one arm across his heart.

The Emperor's secret police
deliberately at the wrong place
shoot aimlessly
at pine trees.
As dusk strains
at the afternoon

the poet, sprawled where
perfect snow bites
at his wound
aims half an age
and hits, though nothing
can rescind his dying now.

The Emperor is vexed
for friends lay out the corpse
in civil dress.

Black liquid's gathered
at the thick lips' corners.
The seconds are arrested
and the horses fed.

Christmas At Bristol

'To behold the death of a child—it is a suffering beyond conception'—Sara Coleridge.
'Little lamb! & the snow would not melt on his limbs!—S. T. Coleridge.

The baby coughed and coughed, clearing its lungs
as of some monstrous hook let down by God.
Sam iced fast in Germany—*Es ist zwar*
ein recht gutes Bier; Wm and Dorothy
not to be found, anonymously siring
the Lucy poems. Ice packed the Elbe,
coldest winter for a hundred years. At one
Sun Feb 10, Berkeley convulsed and died.

Soldiers are blown up or run frenziedly
at death, lust beaming them through
darkness. The old are slowly dragged
past the highest wave. Only the strong
joy of Wm sings total eclipse.
Sara lived it, vein by vein,
hands plucking out the gelid eyes of hope.
Through life she kept the dead birthday.

God is conceived in those High Renaissance
and virgin mothers: they are the rock
on which love hammers and is shod.
To give birth and see the branch sapless
or hacked down—it is a suffering
beyond conception. All light is humbled;
blind snow-glare of the father and the son.

Entering the City with Bliss-Bestowing Hands

Slicing my way through all the shires
I reel in London. Two French girls
hitch-hiking down from Glasgow play
and sing me love songs all the way

and tell me they'll not marry since
all the world claims their allegiance.
Charing Cross Road has starlings, more
than I've ever seen or heard before

needling the streets, then bunching down
to stitch the country to the town.
Next day, in Shaftesbury Avenue, I'm
accosted by a long-lost friend

who's just climbed Nelson's Column, where
he hung a banner in the air
'for freedom'. Over coffee we
rehearse our interim history

since the days we took on Kant and Hume
and who-did-sexually-what-to-whom.
(At graduation, the solitaires
were panicked into sudden pairs

as though the world outside might nail
them singly to a bed-sit wall.)
The evening brings a party, thrown
by refugees from house and home

who've given fame a famished look
and rhymed themselves into a book.
Poets *en masse* are not amusy,
charitable, choice or choosy

so I wander into Chelsea
there to contemplate the species
washed up by the swinging sixties
strolling down the Kings Road sadly.

Next evening, I'm to dine at ten
with spectacular media-men:
one who makes *The Sweeney*, one
an ex- (disastrous) country postman

contracted monthly to the Beeb
who now delivers. Celebrity
has ploughed the blackest rings I've seen
round eyes this side of Gretna Green.

Still, he's taken for his bride
a bouncy make-up girl, high wide
and handsome, just the sort
to put a face on his old hurt.

Next, family; my sister's home
from globetrotting. We pick the bone
of confidences: she's alright
though married to a solemn type

and I'm okay myself, if blessed
with pen and ink and palimpsest.
(My passion's to record; hers is
to break out of parenthesis.)

Driving down to Mother we talk
of books and films and tennis courts
and driving back we analyse
the shifting crafts that shape our lives.

City and country; husband, wife;
the soap that sickles the carving knife.
Wishes flash like neon, desire
is loosely squared in baling wire.

Self-sculpted, monolithic, we stand
attentively as dolmens, mined
by frost and fire and god knows what
deposit in the stony sap.

Enough of talk! Farewell the town's
insomniac and knowing frown.
My car sits at the kerb. I'm off
to the root and the shrub and the Land of Nod.

Icarus

One balm only for the realest hurt
and that's the howl and armour of great art.

The finger in the wound's Emeritus
Professor of High Pain, whose omnibus

excursions round the pit of hell will break
out bloody terror with the chocolate flake.

A smoker's mouth . . . the bitter breath
instantiates the taste of death,

is blurb and prologue. Notwithstanding, I
shall sob your name out at the fells, that high

indifference. Blue haze sits on every rock;
each uttered syllable is volleyed back

the same but different. Look, the river slides
beneath a low stone bridge, green spear-shaped reeds

are trembling in the current, polished stones
banked sweetlier than shingle where cold water bends . . .

It's National Trust, grave metaphor, it's view halloo . . .
These instances are valid too.

The purple's eating up the mountains. Of
great ignorance I speak, and name it love.

Six Bagatelles

i
Chopin would sell his soul
for one heart-breaking chord
and puddle in his own life's blood.
I move another mentioned good:
steel plate to armour love's big ships
at landfall, the high surf
sweet pomp and terror of your lips.

ii
Those ladies of the Regency
indented marble shoulders, left
small classic English breasts
as visiting cards beneath
Mozartian discourse, at home
to such emotions as might thud
across the parquet to love's double doors.

iii
The notes chip at each other like
a man and wife, some ghostly octave
murmuring 'I do . . . I do . . .'
Sonorities: the long view
benched and tested. You remit
this mad baptismal howl of *and*;
kiss my throat lightly with your hand.

iv
Tchaikovsky knew, and look what cries
went hooting round with maddened eyes:
ninety players sobbing out
their hearts upon a city's snout.
Beloved, here be Cheshire grins
patrolling the bridge of violins.

v
(Couplets . . . the very form decrees
we hug each other to our knees
or strike out witty sparks, to light
our hubble-bubble of delight.
I'll love you, love you, love you, till
you sicken of sheer rhyme. Love, Bill.)

vi
Kisses have to be learned
like everything else:
what goes where; which top
you have on; how your hair
beseeches to curl up, and crown
the smile your eyes cannot hold down.
Dear heart, I'm disarmed too. Teach me
interment of this weaponry.

The News

What happens is important, so you lopped
our noise.
            The voices rose, new wavebands, new
inventions. What the papers said, and movies sang,
and TV yammered on the rug, you took in
like an orphan whose affections monitor
each tiny blaze of star. Jerusalem
and wordage, voices in the thick of walls . . .
They stormed across the hearing like another war
and schools sprang up to drill you in the rights
of words.
            Now you've bingo, tribal flocks
of wise old Grans whose shocking feathers
beat out over doorsteps, and a deep-voiced joker
numbers off the ones you didn't want
or wanted last time round. Still you listen,
listen. Politics is pensions, bills, mastectomies,
the one-armed bandit at the door,
it flourishes in chemists and infrequent letters
from your sons. All news will body breath
and pigment of your single state. *No luck*
you whisper down to Dad. Two lemons glowed
right at you; and the high fruit of the lamps.

Our Man at the Bar

George Rand, my masters. And it came to pass
on loan to culture from the working class.

A Thirties baby, rationed, potty-trained,
brought up to Save the King, and to be caned

for insolence (*dumb* insolence) at school,
the Royal High's tradition with a scholar-fool.

Oxford. Loathing shook him like a miner's thirst
in spite of which he took a Double First

and won the Booker with his début, a
post-Beckett, laid-back-Borges exposé

of mental incest ('Powerful' 'Striking' 'Sad')
committed by a high-strung working lad.

More novels, plays, reviews; a large success.
Professors said so in the TLS.

His marriage bust (fame is an awful tart).
George looked within. 'I've played a double part.'

He looked without, took bearings: all his roots
had shifted from the midlands to John Keats,

to Joyce and Lawrence, Orwell's *apercus*:
they loitered in the grounds of Xanadu

where love's great thigh-bone leans into the earth
and hurls off second-raters. Perfect birth

and growth and model failure is its theme.
'I cannot prosper rooted in a dream'

said George; 'besides it's tricky stuff, such glass,
forever condescending to the working class.

Art neutral? Hardly so. The soul of art
is wedded to the fat stipendiary heart

beating its greedy drum above the gut:
tell me who shoves liquor into *that*

and I'll show you which regiment of truth
manoeuvres round the peasant's rotted tooth.'

George turned to verse, new model flint eclogues
honed at his cottage on the Isle of Dogs.

The Hydra head of art, the faceless bland
could reckon now with our man, big George Rand.

The Screes

The screes are speeding down at perfect pitch
before they tuck themselves in envelopes
Wastwater seals and never means to post.
Clouds snuffle by, fat bridesmaids plump with tears.

The screes are swarming up the cliff to lay
their case in heaven. The water's indigo.
A cormorant, wings unpacked, hung out to dry,
stands phoenix-fixed upon a rock. The screes

are drowning out upon the lake, face up.
It rains stops rains; somewhere a bark. The screes
are deep and thinking one emotion through

like Hegel's avalanche of counterpoint
prodding the Absolute to a day's turn.
Sheep press their starter buttons all night long.

The Liquor Cruise

For Tony Brode

Cunard: a masterpiece in black
and white. The big ships butting seawards
like a piece of Dover Cliff.

We cruised and cruised
the fleshpots of the sun, Manhattan
to the nightclub Caribbean.

Bacardi grew me up,
a hot tongue in my ear
somewhere in Kingstown's seedy black.

Nights, our steward's fancy
shorts fetched up at me. He brought
iced melons and Miles Davis

pitching love. On board
six hundred liquor salesmen
boiled from New York State;

they brought their own. I heard
the voices of the dollar bill,
bald eagles stooping to my ear.

Cashed-in like an ice-cube, I
edged up the tall sides
of the pallid flesh

to spend my boyhood
at a single tropic gulp.
Our English officer engineers

emerged from their
inferno scrubbed, immaculate
to dine in white.

Home to the Hudson's broken
ice, the sun a sticker
on each bulging case;

down in my C deck
hovel, the minotaur
good taste!

For Isaac Babel

Well, well, Meander, thou art deeply read;
And having thee, I have a jewel sure.
                    —Marlowe, *Tamburlaine the Great*, II, ii, 55–56

Prestidigitations! Pogroms! Five year plans
for adjectives—for courage, all a man's
fat nerve entailed upon the backbone of a horse
who speaks no Yiddish but has learnt to curse

so many ways he's called a child of God,
God being such a polyvalent clod
The cupolas of churches do not tear
the breast so finely as a bandolier.

And Masha! Such a comfort to the troops
worn out from duty, desultory rapes.
She writes them letters home to Mum, speaks up
for killing prisoners in next day's attack.

One village, then another; these proud Poles
grinding sabres, hooking monocles
up to a frigid eye, are harder work
than cauterising phrases in a book.

One feeling, then another, till they swell
all purple-putrid as a kulak's boil
no-one had thought to lance, till Captain Lvov
rode up and fondly sliced his shoulders off.

Odessa to the Ukraine. One day I read
the Talmud to a Cossack as he bled
to death, pious as a village cat.
Russia? Let her weep. She's good at that

Three From Milton

I. ON THE DEATH OF THE BEADLE OF THE UNIVERSITY OF CAMBRIDGE

(*Elegia secunda, In obitem Praeconsis Academici Cantabriensis.*)

You summoned one and all, your shining mace
the call-sign to Apollo's youthful race;
but Death's a Beadle too, his college door
gapes wider than the womb: and Death said 'More!'
Impervious to senate, court and throne
the Commoner devours his very own.
True, your hair was white, your reverend skin
depended low on each successive chin:
yet you had energy to spare, and might
have lived to bellow Jove himself goodnight,
or eat a goose's liver, reprobate
satiety of years with drunken Yeats.
No need to tell you twice when you were sped
to haul out sloven students from their bed
or rowdy disco, or lubricious benches,
prodigal of high oaths and low wenches.
Staunch as Eurybates, when brought to tell
hothead Achilles of the pains of hell,
or diplomatic Eden, who could chime
out '*Lebensraum*' with 'Peace in our Time'
you, like a seasoned captain, kept your post
between the non-coms and the nabobs. Most,
O Death, this man served those who served the Muse;
why not sweep off some fathead who's no use?
Mourn, therefore, *Academe*: drench the bier
with sounding rhyme, proprietary tear.
Let Elegy, all-purposed, shriek the rules
and statutory endings through our Schools.

2. ON SALMASIUS

(*In Salmasium, Defensio secunda pro Populo Anglicano*)

Hurray for herrings! and the fry that teem
in cold confusion down in *Academe*;
for good Salmasius has undertaken
to save, poor fish! your reputation.
They've made him Knight, he's pricked and kissed
Sir Salmon, a staunch Royalist
who'll blush in any court, and spawn
bad Latin, as to the manner born.
Henceforth you'll wear his livery, my smart fish,
all frilled and furbelowed upon the dish.
Death with honour! and a boon to these
who wipe their noses on their sleeve.

3. ON THE GUNPOWDER PLOT

(In Proditionem Bombardicam)

So this was how to harness hell's own flames
and levitate the body of King James,
you skulking monsters? Revolution! But
each Brutus holds the knife at his own gut;
a traitor's reason stomachs all the odds
except the stigma of its plaster gods.
Without your hellish help, he's lately given
the last of's audiences to friendly heaven.
How you'll get there God knows! unless you buy
indulgences for teaching men to fly
and pray a little, now that our late James
disputes not Roman nor revisionist flames.

Small Event on the Chaise Longue

The black cat stretches up its arching neck
paws braced on airy nothing (midnight trips
some ancient racial memory); submits
to slump back to his cauldron ring of peace,
tail, paws and pointed face
all coinciding in one peaceful place.

Relaxed as any drunk; ascending higher
on simple warmth than Joan of Arc on fire.
They've only got one word, and that's *miaow*:
which crops them quicker food than any plough.
Their body is their syntax. In one move
is coiled the very slug and root of love.

Wishbone

My wish is simple, Lord, though open to
derision. I should like to see my hips
swell out a bit, and of their own volition mix
up courtly motions in my skirt, as You
presumably ordained; and feel it right
to wear those tiny nether garments in Your sight.

Concomitant on that, I'd like to smell
of roses of Arabia, and fold
the archaeology of love in cold
and fleshly audit, rather as the fell
administers its weathers. Let me cease
spotting the blemish in the human face.

The thought that men are incidental to
the solemn mysteries—*viz*. birth—goes hard,
though envy's not my motive. The petard
I want to choke on's more to do
with provenance, the inside rationale,
placenta to that Gioconda smile.

Well, if not literal flesh and blood, I hope
to bring back traces of a gentler birth
though it may be that vatic Mother Earth
is hard as nails, and various as rope.
But sure I'll be less as a sounding brass—
and more forthcoming than Tiresias!

Humbug detectors, bottomless yearnings, I
look forward most to meeting in my breast
some nameless arctic leopard, atavist
and poet, built to cleanse the eye
of dreams, kick up the snow a little, lease
each sinew to the ice-cap, and lie down in peace.

The Visit

Her ageing mother sits with knees apart
smiling at circumstance. She
never owned a room like this, nor
wildcat feelings either. Freedom?
If a man lapped at the bowl of love
you held it up for blessing, placed
a household thirsting at the hungry breast.
What pride is lugged from childhood—
each step must be good, each good
a better than was known before.
Who hasn't greased the stomach of desire?
Yet thoughts, to those who've thought them,
turn out much the same, a doctor's bag
to send the world far off
and bring it back just one day at a time.
So, distant on a higher stair, she aims
her smile between expensive furniture,
new books, that agitated cigarette
whose smoke goes blueing up, contracting
now with nothing much, one white hand
hauling on the banister's fine grain.

Night Music

Failed marriages, lip service to desire
and rabid formulae of Petrarch now are
retailed by the saxaphone, a bent guitar.

Don't turn your nose up. Cisterns flow,
incise entailments, cry *reductio*
wherever there's a tranny and a lady-O.

The Raid

Your stomach, love, 's a crock of gold;
two dragon hips; your ruined breast
a warrior's empty cache of spears.
Great longboat, you have sunk to rest

and sea-changed there I flicker through
magnificence, the grain laid bare.
All's silent, livid, prideless. How
far sunlight hacks the upper air!

Executive Estate

'*The admiration of mountains is an invention of protestantism . . . If of the tree the mountains make a fir, you can imagine what they can do with man . . . The fir and the palm tree: those two extremes.*'

—André Gide, *Journals*

At dusk these gardens bleed with neatness.
Bed, bush and sward, a soldier's kit
squared off beneath the wide-eyed moon.

Last week young mothers zoned their parts
out on the grass, raised up on lilos
from each mortgaged strip of worms.

Putting sex to work or play is exercise
for someone. Shall we pelt the East
with payslips and mute conifers

or set each Parliament to stone
the lewd, hair-raising limbs of dates?
Yet Antony was fertile of a most unRoman

blush; and in our time compassion stalks
the embassies in Savanarola hoods.
If heaven is an English lawn

and clumps of gaitered beeches, guzzling
calm, then all these rakes
and mowers propagate a holy war

where secateurs and pesticides
out-ravish all the blunt-eyed whores
moistening their subsoils two spits down.

(The old go down in black and white
each shut eye clamorous
as a made bed . . .)

As for the houses, André, they are dull
and neuter, deserts of pale bradstone
trying out heroic names.

Marriage Song

I

It was that dressing-gown, deep medieval blue
and starred with tiny flowers, that did for me.
Hair up, fresh from the bath, you stood there
like a book of hours. It was a charity

in me to take confession of those breasts
and rosy nipples, of the clasping root
that split old grimy London head to foot,
and nail the clamour of your lips. Alas!

I am of them that snuffle up small pint
and range the world in transubstantial books
which armours me against small deaths but not,
it seems, this odyssey of killing looks.

II

In Hampstead, on the tilt, repeating word
for word our promptings, looking up to see
the solemn paradigms, a family
which mingled hope and pain as something stirred
and broke the surface of them all, we said
the word and walked out smiling. Photographs
snatched by a friend showed later that you'd cried
at first, balancing the bride
in you against the funeral of a girl
who'd left blood on the landscape, run amok
to lock out accidentals. It took
two continents to grow you: now you move
into the narrow orbit of sheer love
high up above them all, where comets shine
and men rehearse quotations, all space-time
bent round in adoration now we cut
and cast the skin we lived in, as the moon comes up.

Ice for the Lips

Ice for the lips, pain in the wordless mouth.

Beneath one brittle hood the skin had thicked.
He cried out when I cut his nails, as you
might cry, in fear of what my loving lacked,
as my life sliced your own: a perfect O
and Christ! of tender cursing. So
the night-nurse thundered on the window
of our vigil. Christmas Day. She pulled
and straightened him like a starched table cloth.

The Knot

No-one heard your breathing stop
that dark dawn
for the living must sleep
and though our best selves overtop
division, I should like to have known
the line was drawn.

Clamour of mirrors, devout
silence, breath
lunging at each mouth. The lover
in us rouses: sends out
to call in—his torrid debt—
immaculate, the plaited wreath.

Ronsard, I.i

Helen, this is the first of May. I swear
by Castor, Pollux, your two heavenly twins;
blunt tender vines that lace about the elms;
by all that's building castles in the air;

by spring, by procreation, by the streams
that croon and loose their braids; by nightingales
sobbing aloud their sweet demented trills,
you are the inhalation of my dreams.

You only please me: compos mentis, I,
a balancer of virtues, choose to serve
and sweat my chance on love's minutiae.

To bend the knee to flesh! It's madness, it's
the primrose path to ruin. This I pledge:
your breasts shall nail me to my crucifix!

On The Move

At Euston Concourse, Lord, a black girl stacked
up six foot six in a queue that snaked
across great marble floors. Curled dreadlocks
swung; her satin rocket launcher jeans
were tongues of fire, and the air burnt all
around. In my queue soared a white girl
bound in classic blue, breasts slung to point
a simple cotton blouse. Their faces are
soft hangings, pale ambiguous walls to flex
in space: and which is out or in no man
can say. Body and brains in the bookshops,
Lord, in restaurants and galleries such
ardours and perfections joint the eye:
time-lapsed film of the petals rushing by.

And hunger is a journey, Lord, to ride
in your soft cities, and hard countryside.

Hugh MacDiarmid Goes to Heaven

Deil amang ye knowed a thocht but me.
Whae's to poor ma whisky noo? Get out
ma road, ye loon-faced spricht! Nae, tak
me up tae Lenin's lodgins first
then mebbe I'll hae words wi your peedie God
gin He dosnae hum an haw in Oxfoord cant.
Eternity is like an auld green parrot
I said aince. (Ye hae your Hamletisms
an I hae mine.) It goes hard but this braw scrunt
dosnae lend th'old buzzard a wee bit lurch
an whummle the couthie richt aff o his perch!

The Small Rain

'*was never non but che*'

Wake to the bone's return wake to this face
The bare branch sets his standard in this place

Soft pulse of flesh-fat fields A storied rain
collects remorseless through each bloodied vein

Wake to remembered eyes be lucid there
light struts, or tangles our bright harvester

Let red lips grip you let the body kiss
Was never love died slept the soul Souls miss

their docking, once drift helpless to all space
void, featureless Love, set your carapace

down surely crew me glutted tears, huge skies
to hurtle out of this world only to the wise

The Consecration

I see you in your kitchen, sunny-clear,
reading, as in a painting by Vermeer.

I see you tilt your face, to take the weight
of world's wide admiration, or dilate

that diamond-point of will, set deep in sighs,
to charm the willing, and assuage the wise.

I see you bowl past in your Renault car
reverberant as a steel guitar.

I see you with your Roxy music, Strauss,
Purcell and Schubert, wheeling round the house

or captaining the ironing board, Pietà of
the sheets and shirts, wrapped in a fierce diurnal love.

I see you taking classes, getting A's.
I hear your teachers at their Marseillaise.

I taste you in the whole foods, in boutiques,
I hear the very zip and how it shrieks . . .

and watch you light the mirror with a smile
of maculate self-knowledge, maiden guile.

I see you ache with beauty, and I read
in your bared shoulders, beauty is betrayed,

the bow each man might bend. I see
exile and madness on the wine-dark sea.

I see that rain's eternal—mad eclipse
of sun and season in those summary lips.

(Rain is your element: you said so, hand
in hand with the bright lakes of Cumberland.)

I watch you re-write Milton, Genesis,
the mad misogyny of feminists

and note the laughter-lines, the calmest joy
since all the heroines of Lev Tolstoy.

I see you far and near, in myth, in dream,
the Maja's granite noun, love's twinned phoneme,

Natasha, Anna, Sonya . . . train and track . . .
imagination's hugest, blankest cheque!

I see you sinking down amid the mess
of kids; I see you armed with tenderness.

I see my seeing has a lover's tongue . . .
to dead-head all the prophets . . . dead . . . dead-wrong.